The Pocket Rune Reset

The Pocket Rune Reset

M J MEREDITH

CONTENTS

DEDICATION	vi
Introduction	1
Section1: How to Use This Booklet	5
Section2: Rune-by-Rune Quick Meditations	7
Section 3: Quick Reference Guide	59
Bonus: The Science of Stillness at Work	61
YOUR "RESET" IN PRACTICE	65
FURTHER READING/OTHER RESOURCES	69

When we are lost, the universe sometimes sends us guides—souls whose hearts and minds, without reason or reward, simply choose to show the way. Sometimes they arrive as a single shining light, and we feel fortunate to know them. Sometimes they come in tandem, a duo whose presence feels like a rare and precious gift. And on the rarest of occasions, they appear as an entire organisation, where vision and wisdom combine to create something extraordinary.

I have been blessed to know them all.

To Kimberlie and Julian, whose guidance has been a beacon, and to ETC, whose collective spirit has illuminated the journey—may your light continue to guide, uplift, and inspire all who cross your path.

Copyright © 2025 by M J MEREDITH
All rights reserved. No part of this book may be reproduced in any manner whatsoever without written permission except in the case of brief quotations embodied in critical articles and reviews.
First Printing, 2025
Paperback 978-1-7642012-7-8
E book 978-1-7642012-8-5

Introduction

Acknowledging busyness in modern life.

In today's fast-paced world, it can feel like there's never a moment to pause. Emails pile up, meetings blur together, and the pressure to perform can leave even the most organised professional stretched thin. Sound familiar? This mini guide is designed for those stolen moments — the few quiet minutes at your desk, or even during your commute. It's for when you need a reset. The exercises and reflections here, inspired by the ancient wisdom of the runes, will help you find calm, clarity, and balance, even in the middle of a hectic workday.

"Sound familiar?"

Why mindfulness matters in business.

Mindfulness isn't just a wellness trend; it's a practical tool for navigating the challenges of modern business. Taking even a few moments to centre yourself can sharpen focus, improve decision-making, and unlock creativity — while reducing stress and the risk of burnout. By cultivating awareness and presence, you respond thoughtfully rather than react impulsively, communicate more effectively, and stay resilient in the face of setbacks. Mindfulness equips you to lead, work, and create with clarity and intention, turning even brief pauses into powerful moments of balance.

"What would your workday look like if you felt calmer and clearer?"

How runes, as ancient symbols, can act as powerful anchors.

Runes are more than ancient symbols; they are tools of reflection, focus, and insight that have guided thought and action for centuries. In this booklet, each rune acts as a simple anchor for your attention, a focal point during moments of pause. By drawing on their symbolic meanings, you can quickly shift your mindset, clarify your intentions, and ground yourself amid the constant demands of work. Think of them as tiny beacons in your pocket — ready to help you reconnect with calm, perspective, and purpose whenever you need it.

"Could a simple symbol become your anchor in the chaos?"

> "This isn't about hours of practice. It's about short, practical moments to reset."

Section 1: How to Use This Booklet

This guide is designed to be flexible, practical, and easy to weave into even the busiest schedule. There's no "right" way to use it — only what works best for you.

Option 1: Let Intuition Lead

Open the booklet at random and allow the rune you land on to guide your reflection. Sometimes the message you most need is the one you weren't expecting. (Section 2 Rune-by-Rune Quick Meditations)

Option 2: Choose with Intention

If you're facing a specific challenge. A stressful meeting, a tight deadline, or a difficult decision, select the rune that aligns with the guidance or energy you need most. (Section 3 Quick Reference Guide)

Suggested Daily or Weekly Practices

- **Morning Reset:** Spend 3–5 minutes with a rune before your day begins. Reflect on its meaning, use the quick affirmation, and set your intention.
- **Pre-Meeting Pause:** Take a moment with a rune as a grounding exercise before a key discussion or presentation.
- **End-of-Day Reflection:** Revisit the rune of the day and jot down how its message showed up in your work, choices, or interactions.

Even just a few mindful minutes can provide clarity, reduce stress, and help you approach work with greater calm and focus. The key is consistency. Small pauses add up to meaningful shifts in balance and perspective.

Section2: Rune-by-Rune Quick Meditations

**This Rune Represents
"Success in Business"**

Fehu – Wealth, Flow & Abundance

Theme: Prosperity, resources, and energy flow in business

Business Perspective: Managing resources wisely, recognising value, and creating sustainable growth.

Business-Focused Affirmation: "I welcome the flow of resources and opportunities. I use my energy and time with clarity, aligning my actions with growth and prosperity."

Quick Meditation (3–5 minutes):
Find a quiet moment and take three steady breaths. Visualise the symbol of Fehu glowing softly before you, radiating calm, golden energy. Imagine this energy flowing toward you as streams of resources — time, creativity, support, and opportunities. See these resources weaving into your work with balance and purpose, strengthening focus and direction.

Silently repeat: *"I allow abundance to flow into my work. I act with clarity and calm."*

Reflection Prompt:

- Where am I blocking flow or resisting support?
- What small step today could invite greater abundance and ease into my work?
- How can I share resources to strengthen my team or community?

Uruz – Strength, Vitality & Resilience

Theme: Personal power, stamina, and resilience in the face of challenges

Business Perspective: Building resilience, sustaining energy, and having the courage to move through obstacles.

Business-Focused Affirmation: "I draw on my inner strength. I meet challenges with calm determination, knowing I have the resilience to keep moving forward."

Quick Meditation (3–5 minutes):
Sit comfortably and take a few steady breaths. Visualise the symbol of Uruz glowing steadily before you. Imagine its energy flowing into your body, filling you with grounded strength and clear focus. Feel it steadying your nerves and renewing your determination to face today's tasks.

Silently repeat: *"I stand resilient and balanced. I meet challenges with clarity and strength."*

Reflection Prompt:

- Where in my work do I need more endurance or patience?
- Which obstacles feel overwhelming, and how can I break them into smaller steps?
- How can I balance persistence with calm focus today?

Thurisaz – Protection, Boundaries & Clarity

Theme: Setting limits, making wise choices, and protecting your energy.

Business Perspective: Risk awareness, boundary setting, learning from obstacles.

Business-Focused Affirmation: "I protect my energy and focus. I set clear boundaries and approach challenges with wisdom and clarity."

Quick Meditation (3–5 minutes):

Sit comfortably and take a few deep breaths. Visualise Thurisaz glowing before you, its sharp energy forming a protective shield around your mind and workspace. Imagine this shield filtering distractions, stress, and unnecessary demands, leaving you with clarity for what matters most.

Silently repeat: *"I act with clarity. I maintain strong boundaries and protect my focus."*

Reflection Prompt:

- Where in my work do I need stronger boundaries?
- Which distractions or obligations can I release today?
- How can I stand firm in my priorities without conflict?

Ansuz – Communication & Insight

Theme: Clear expression, guidance, and creative thinking.

Business Perspective: Honest communication, active listening, learning from mentors, and sharing ideas effectively.

Business-Focused Affirmation:
"I communicate with clarity and listen with presence. I share ideas openly and welcome insight that guides my decisions."

Quick Meditation (3–5 minutes):
Sit comfortably and breathe deeply. Visualise Ansuz glowing softly before you, like an open channel of light. Imagine this light clearing pathways for words, ideas, and understanding — between yourself, your team, and your inner wisdom. Feel the calm confidence that comes when communication flows effortlessly.

Silently repeat: *"I listen deeply. I speak with intention. I act with insight."*

Reflection Prompt:

- Where could clearer communication improve outcomes in my work?
- How can I listen today to truly understand, not just respond?
- What message, idea, or piece of guidance am I ready to share?

Raido – Journey & Progress

Theme: Purposeful movement, steady progress, and adaptability.

Business Perspective: Strategic planning, taking intentional steps forward, and embracing change as part of the process.

Business-Focused Affirmation: "I move forward with clarity and purpose. I embrace each stage of the journey, adapting with confidence and staying focused on progress."

Quick Meditation (3–5 minutes):
Sit comfortably, take a few deep breaths, and visualise Raido as a guiding path stretching before you. See yourself walking steadily along it, each step deliberate and calm. Allow any anxiety about deadlines or uncertainty to fade, replaced by trust in the process and your ability to keep moving forward.

Silently repeat: *"I progress with purpose. I adapt with ease. I trust the journey."*

Reflection Prompt:

- Where am I resisting progress or holding back in my work?
- What one small, intentional step can I take today to move closer to my goals?
- How can I stay present and focused on the process, not just the outcome?

Kenaz – Insight, Creativity & Illumination

Theme: Clarity of thought, fresh ideas, and innovative solutions.

Business Perspective: Sparking creativity, problem-solving, and shining light on opportunities that may have been overlooked.

Business-Focused Affirmation: "I welcome clarity and creativity. I see new possibilities with confidence and act on them with inspired intention."

Quick Meditation (3–5 minutes):

Find a calm space and take steady breaths. Visualise Kenaz as a glowing flame, casting warm light over your mind and workspace. Feel this light illuminating challenges, revealing solutions, and sparking creative ideas. Allow yourself to feel energised by the clarity and vision it brings.

Silently repeat: *"I see with clarity. I create with confidence. I act with inspired purpose."*

Reflection Prompt:

- What challenge in my work could benefit from a fresh perspective?
- How can I let creativity guide my decision-making today?
- What small step can I take to bring light to my next opportunity?

Gebo – Collaboration, Balance & Reciprocity

Theme: Partnerships, exchange, and mutual benefit.

Business Perspective: Building trust, fostering collaboration, and ensuring fair, balanced exchanges in professional relationships.

Business-Focused Affirmation: "I give and receive support with balance. I nurture collaboration that creates mutual benefit, trust, and harmony in my work."

Quick Meditation (3–5 minutes):
Take a few deep breaths and visualise Gebo, its simple cross shape symbolising balance and exchange. Imagine a flow of energy between yourself and those you work with — colleagues, clients, or partners. Feel the balance of giving and receiving, recognising that true collaboration is built on trust, fairness, and respect.

Silently repeat: *"I cultivate balance in relationships. I give and receive support with integrity and openness."*

Reflection Prompt:

- Where in my work could stronger collaboration improve outcomes?
- How can I offer support without overextending myself?
- Who can I invite into partnership to create more balance and success?

Wunjo – Joy, Satisfaction & Wellbeing

Theme: Positive energy, fulfilment, and motivation in work

Business Perspective: Workplace morale, celebrating wins, creating positive energy.

Business-Focused Affirmation: "I embrace the joy in my work. I celebrate successes, cultivate positive energy, and allow harmony to guide interactions with my team and clients."

Quick Meditation (3–5 minutes):
Take a grounding breath and bring the rune's shape to mind. Visualise Wunjo glowing brightly, radiating warmth and joy throughout your mind and workspace. Feel satisfaction and positive energy filling your day, even in small moments of accomplishment.

Silently repeat: *"I invite joy and fulfillment into my work. I notice and celebrate small successes."*

Reflection Prompt:

- What aspect of my work brings me genuine satisfaction today?
- How can I infuse more joy or lightness into my tasks?
- Which small wins can I acknowledge to boost motivation and wellbeing?

Hagalaz – Change, Challenges & Transformation

Theme: Embracing disruption, adapting with resilience

Business Perspective: Embracing change, turning setbacks into growth, resilience.

Business-Focused Affirmation: "I welcome change and disruption as a path to growth. I release fear and remain adaptable, turning obstacles into lessons and opportunities for transformation."

Quick Meditation (3–5 minutes):
Close your eyes and let the rune's energy settle into your awareness. Visualise Hagalaz glowing, its energy representing both challenge and transformation. Accept that change is part of business and life, and allow yourself to see obstacles as opportunities for growth.

Silently repeat: *"I embrace change with resilience. I transform challenges into opportunities."*

Reflection Prompt:

- What current challenge could I reframe as a learning opportunity?
- Where might flexibility help me move forward with ease?
- How can I stay grounded during unexpected changes?

Nauthiz – Necessity, Patience & Constraint

Theme: Managing limitations, prioritising, and patience

Business Perspective: Prioritisation, dealing with limitations, mindful decision-making.

Business-Focused Affirmation: "I acknowledge limitations without judgement. I focus on priorities, make deliberate choices, and use constraints as a guide for smarter decision-making."

Quick Meditation (3–5 minutes):

Focus on your breathing until calm arrives, then visualise Nauthiz glowing softly. Let its energy remind you that constraints can create focus and clarity. Reflect on what is essential today and where patience can guide better decisions.

Silently repeat: *"I work with patience and purpose. I prioritise what truly matters."*

Reflection Prompt:

- Which tasks or demands can I prioritise and which can I release?
- Where can patience improve my decision-making today?
- How can I turn limitations into opportunities for focus?

Isa – Stillness, Clarity & Pause

Theme: Calm, reflection, and regaining perspective

Business Perspective: Reflection, patience, avoiding impulsive decisions, clarity of mind.

Business-Focused Affirmation: "I pause and breathe, creating space to think clearly. I resist rushing, allowing stillness to bring insight and grounded decisions in my business life."

Quick Meditation (3–5 minutes):
Sit quietly and visualise Isa, a still, vertical line glowing gently. Let its presence slow your mind, bringing clarity and calm. Use this moment to pause, breathe, and regain perspective on your work and priorities.

Silently repeat: *"I embrace stillness. I gain clarity and perspective in every moment."*

Reflection Prompt:

- Where in my day do I need a pause to regain clarity?
- How can stillness help me make wiser decisions?
- What distractions can I release to restore calm?

Jera – Cycles, Progress & Rewards

Theme: Patience, timing, and recognising growth

Business Perspective: Recognising cycles, patience for results, measuring progress. Valuing the importance of analysing project cycles or quarterly outcomes.

Business-Focused Affirmation: "I reflect on the work I've done and the outcomes I seek. I trust in timing and cycles, patiently nurturing my projects until they yield their results."

Quick Meditation (3–5 minutes): Visualise Jera glowing and turning slowly, representing cycles and natural progression. Reflect on recent efforts and the outcomes that are emerging. Recognise that steady, thoughtful work brings rewards over time.

Silently repeat: *"I trust the timing of my work. I honour progress and growth."*

Reflection Prompt:

- What recent efforts am I ready to acknowledge or celebrate?
- How can I stay patient while awaiting outcomes?
- What small actions today contribute to long-term success?

Eihwaz – Resilience, Endurance & Protection

Theme: Strength in adversity, grounding, and safeguarding energy

Business Perspective: Long-term planning, persistence through difficulty, inner strength.

Business-Focused Affirmation: "I stand firm in the face of challenges. I draw on inner endurance and protective focus, maintaining steady progress even when obstacles arise."

Quick Meditation (3–5 minutes):
Close your eyes and let the rune's energy settle into your awareness of Eihwaz, a steady, protective energy. Feel its strength supporting you as you face challenges, helping you endure difficulties without losing balance or calm.

Silently repeat: *"I stand strong and resilient. I protect my energy and maintain balance."*

Reflection Prompt:

- Where in my work do I need to cultivate resilience?
- How can I maintain balance under pressure?
- What protective boundaries can I set to preserve focus and energy?

Perthro – Opportunity, Potential & Discovery

Theme: Embracing unknown possibilities, intuition, and creativity

Business Perspective: Risk-taking, embracing the unknown, trusting intuition.

Business-Focused Affirmation: "I embrace uncertainty as opportunity. I trust intuition, explore new ventures with curiosity, and allow unexpected possibilities to guide growth."

Quick Meditation (3–5 minutes):
Take a grounding breath and bring Perthro's shape to mind, representing hidden opportunities waiting to be discovered. Open your mind to possibilities in your work and trust your intuition to guide you toward the right path.

Silently repeat: *"I welcome opportunity and embrace potential. I trust my intuition to guide me."*

Reflection Prompt:

- Where in my work could I explore new opportunities?
- How can I cultivate curiosity and openness today?
- What potential outcome am I ready to pursue with confidence?

Algiz – Protection, Support & Awareness

Theme: Safeguarding energy, setting boundaries, and cultivating awareness

Business Perspective: Boundaries, self-care, seeking guidance, safeguarding wellbeing.

Business-Focused Affirmation: "I feel a shield of support around my business and myself. I protect what is valuable, seek guidance when needed, and move forward confidently."

Quick Meditation (3–5 minutes):

Close your eyes and visualise Algiz glowing brightly, forming a protective shield around your mind and workspace. Feel safe, supported, and able to focus clearly on what truly matters.

Silently repeat: *"I protect my energy and maintain awareness. I act with clarity and calm."*

Reflection Prompt:

- Where do I need to reinforce boundaries today?
- How can I maintain awareness of my energy and priorities?
- Which situations require extra care or focus to protect my wellbeing?

Sowilo – Success, Clarity & Positive Energy

Theme: Motivation, accomplishment, and optimism

Business Perspective: Achieving goals, motivation, clarity, driving forward with purpose.

Business-Focused Affirmation: "I visualise success and positive outcomes. I energise my actions with clarity, focus, and purposeful drive, moving toward goals with confidence."

Quick Meditation (3–5 minutes): Sit quietly and visualise Sowilo shining like a guiding sun, energising your mind and workspace. Let its warmth inspire confidence, optimism, and clarity as you approach your tasks.

Silently repeat: *"I embrace clarity and positivity. I approach my work with energy and purpose."*

Reflection Prompt:

- What tasks today would benefit from renewed energy and optimism?
- How can I cultivate a positive outlook in challenging situations?
- What successes, however small, can I celebrate today?

Tiwaz – Leadership, Courage & Purpose

Theme: Confident decision-making, ethical action, and focused intention

Business Perspective: Ethical decisions, responsibility, accountability, courage to lead.

Business-Focused Affirmation: "I embody leadership with integrity. I make fair, ethical decisions and take responsibility for my choices, guiding my business with courage and clarity."

Quick Meditation (3–5 minutes):
Sit comfortably and visualise Tiwaz glowing, its arrow guiding you toward confident, purposeful decisions. Feel courage and clarity fill your mind as you approach your work with integrity and intention.

Silently repeat: *"I act with courage and purpose. I make decisions with clarity and integrity."*

Reflection Prompt:

- Which decisions today require courage and clarity?
- How can I lead with intention and integrity in my work?
- What steps can I take to act confidently while staying balanced?

Berkano – Growth, Nurturing & Renewal

Theme: Personal and professional development, fostering potential

Business Perspective: Personal development, learning, nurturing ideas or teams.

Business-Focused Affirmation: "I nurture growth in my business and myself. I embrace learning, support development, and welcome renewal after challenges or setbacks."

Quick Meditation (3–5 minutes):

Take a grounding breath and bring Berkano to mind. Nurture your ideas and projects as you would a high-potential venture—giving structure, support, and focus to help them thrive. Let its energy guide steady growth, patience, and attention to what matters most.

Silently repeat: *"I nurture my growth and the growth of my work. I approach challenges with patience and care."*

Reflection Prompt:

- Which projects or relationships need nurturing today?
- How can I encourage growth in myself and others?
- Where can patience help me achieve better outcomes?

Ehwaz – Partnership, Movement & Progress

Theme: Collaboration, trust, and forward momentum

Business Perspective: Teamwork, trust, moving forward together, supporting others.

Business-Focused Affirmation: "I move forward with trusted partners. I cultivate trust, collaboration, and progress, recognising that teamwork strengthens outcomes."

Quick Meditation (3–5 minutes):

Focus on your breathing until calm arrives, then visualise Ehwaz glowing, representing a strong and reliable partnership. Feel energy flowing smoothly, helping you move forward with trust and cooperation.

Silently repeat: *"I cultivate trust and collaboration. I move forward with clarity and purpose."*

Reflection Prompt:

- Where could collaboration improve outcomes today?
- How can I build trust in my work relationships?
- What small steps can I take to maintain progress with confidence?

Mannaz – Humanity, Self & Community

Theme: Self-awareness, teamwork, and mindful leadership

Business Perspective: Self-awareness, collaboration, understanding human dynamics.

Business-Focused Affirmation: "I reflect on my role within my team and community. I foster self-awareness and empathy, enhancing collaboration and understanding in all relationships."

Quick Meditation (3–5 minutes):

Sit quietly and visualise Mannaz glowing, connecting your awareness of self with others around you. Reflect on how your actions and presence impact your team, clients, and community.

Silently repeat: *"I honour myself and others. I act with awareness and integrity in all interactions."*

Reflection Prompt:

- How can I contribute positively to my team or community today?
- Where could greater self-awareness improve my decisions or interactions?
- What qualities in myself do I want to bring forward in my work?

Laguz – Flow, Intuition & Adaptability

Theme: Going with the flow, trusting instincts, and staying flexible

Business Perspective: Adaptability, going with the flow, trusting instincts.

Business-Focused Affirmation: "I allow intuition and natural flow to guide decisions. I trust the timing of events and adapt fluidly, moving with the rhythm of opportunities."

Quick Meditation (3–5 minutes): Visualise Laguz glowing like a flowing river, guiding your mind to trust intuition and remain adaptable. Allow challenges to be met with calm, flowing responses rather than resistance. See yourself adapting to market shifts or client needs.

Silently repeat: *"I trust my intuition. I move with the flow and adapt with ease."*

Reflection Prompt:

- Where in my work could I be more flexible or adaptable?
- How can I better trust my instincts today?
- What small change could improve the flow of my day?

Inguz – Potential, Fertility & New Beginnings

Theme: Starting new projects, seizing opportunities, and creative energy

Business Perspective: New projects, seizing opportunities, latent potential ready to emerge.

Business-Focused Affirmation: "I see potential in projects and ideas. I nurture new beginnings with care, allowing energy and innovation to grow and flourish."

Quick Meditation (3–5 minutes):
Sit comfortably and visualise Inguz glowing with potential, representing new ideas and beginnings. Feel energy building for projects or initiatives ready to be born.

Silently repeat: *"I welcome new opportunities and embrace creative potential. I take inspired action."*

Reflection Prompt:

- Which ideas am I ready to bring to life?
- How can I nurture potential projects or opportunities today?
- Where can I take inspired action in my work?

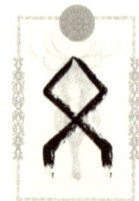

Othala – Legacy, Values & Ownership

Theme: Long-term vision, integrity, and what you leave behind

Business Perspective: Values, legacy, grounding, long-term security, brand values and business legacy.

Business-Focused Affirmation: "I draw strength from roots, values, and legacy. I make decisions grounded in stability while honouring long-term goals and traditions."

Quick Meditation (3–5 minutes): Visualise Othala glowing steadily, connecting your actions today with the long-term impact they create. Reflect on the values guiding your decisions and the legacy you are building in your work.

Silently repeat: *"I act with integrity and purpose. I build a legacy aligned with my values."*

Reflection Prompt:

- What long-term impact do I want to create through my work?
- Are my daily actions aligned with my values?
- How can I ensure my work contributes positively to others and the future?

Dagaz – Breakthrough, Clarity & Transformation

Theme: Achievement, illumination, and new perspectives

Business Perspective: Breakthroughs, clarity after struggle, embracing new beginnings.

Business-Focused Affirmation: "I am open to breakthroughs and clarity. I release old patterns that no longer serve me, embracing new beginnings and transformative opportunities."

Quick Meditation (3–5 minutes):
Sit quietly and visualise Dagaz glowing brightly, marking a breakthrough or moment of insight. Let its light illuminate solutions, reveal opportunities, and energise your perspective.

Silently repeat: *"I embrace breakthroughs and new perspectives. I approach challenges with clarity and balance."*

Reflection Prompt:

- What insight or breakthrough am I ready to receive today?
- Where can I gain clarity to move forward more effectively?
- How can I apply new perspectives to improve my work and wellbeing?

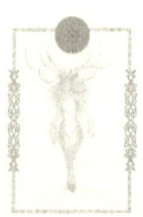

Odin's Rune (Wyrd Rune) – Fate, Insight & Personal Guidance

Theme: Connection to intuition, purpose, and the flow of opportunities

Business Perspective: strategic foresight, intuition, and navigating uncertainty.

Business-Focused Affirmation: "I trust my intuition and insight. I see opportunities clearly and navigate uncertainty with confidence, aligning each decision with my long-term vision and purpose."

Quick Meditation (3–5 minutes):
Sit quietly and take slow, deep breaths. Visualise Odin's Rune glowing, a symbol of guidance and insight connecting you to both your inner wisdom and the opportunities unfolding around you. Feel a sense of calm as you trust the flow of events, knowing you are guided in your decisions and actions.

Silently repeat: *"I trust the guidance of my intuition. I act with purpose and embrace the opportunities before me."*

Reflection Prompt:

- Where in my work could I trust my intuition more fully?
- How can I recognise and act on opportunities aligned with my purpose?
- What guidance or insight am I ready to receive today to support my decisions?

"Mindfulness isn't about clearing your mind — it's about noticing what's already there."

Section 3: Quick Reference Guide

Rune	Name	Keywords	Rune	Name	Keywords
ᚠ	Fehu	Wealth, Abundance	ᛇ	Eihwaz	Endurance, Protection
ᚢ	Uruz	Strength, Vitality	ᛈ	Perthro	Mystery, Opportunity
ᚦ	Thurisaz	Challenge, Protection	ᛉ	Algiz	Protection, Support
ᚨ	Ansuz	Communication, Wisdom	ᛋ	Sowilo	Success, Energy
ᚱ	Raido	Journey, Movement	ᛏ	Tiwaz	Leadership, Justice
ᚲ	Kenaz	Creativity, Vision	ᛒ	Berkano	Growth, Renewal
ᚷ	Gebo	Partnership, Balance	ᛖ	Ehwaz	Partnership, Progress
ᚹ	Wunjo	Joy, Harmony	ᛗ	Mannaz	Self, Community
ᚺ	Hagalaz	Disruption, Transformation	ᛚ	Laguz	Flow, Intuition
ᚾ	Nauthiz	Necessity, Constraint	ᛜ	Inguz	Fertility, Potential
ᛁ	Isa	Stillness, Pause	ᛟ	Othala	Heritage, Stability
ᛃ	Jera	Harvest, Results	ᛞ	Dagaz	Breakthrough, Transformation
Blank Rune	Odin's Rune	Fate, Insight & Personal Guidance			

"The present moment is the only time over which we have dominion."

Thích Nhất Hạnh

Bonus: The Science of Stillness at Work

(This bonus section is a cut down excerpt from my book Runes for Mindfulness: a Guide to Inner Peace.)

"Skeptical? Good. Mindfulness doesn't ask for belief, just attention."

You've probably flicked through this little guide and maybe are still wondering, does this actually do anything?

So for that part of your brain that wants evidence. Here is a brief look at the neuroscience and psychology of mindfulness. No fluff, just facts and how they support the kind of rune-based reflection this book offers.

What Happens in the Brain During Mindfulness?

1. Your Amygdala (emotional alarm system) Calms Down. - It detects threats and ramps up fear and anxiety. Being that our everyday world is constantly stressful, it overreacts. Mindfulness practices reduce activity in the amygdala, helping you stay calm under pressure. The result? Less reactivity, more emotional stability, and a better ability to pause before you pounce.

2. Your Prefrontal Cortex (the decision-making centre) Lights Up - It handles empathy, planning, and emotional regulation. Mindfulness strengthens this area, especially the part responsible for self-awareness and impulse control. That's why, over time, regular mindfulness makes you more focused, more compassionate, and less likely to lose it when life throws curve-balls.

3. Your Vagus Nerve Switches On - The vagus nerve runs from your brain down through your heart, lungs, and gut. It's like your body's internal peacekeeper. When you breathe deeply or settle into calm awareness, this nerve kicks in—slowing your heart rate, reducing inflammation, and turning on your "rest and digest" mode. Mindful breathing and visualisation stimulate the vagus nerve, helping your entire system return to balance. Even in the middle of chaos.

Why Symbols Like Runes Actually Work

Symbols and rituals aren't fluff. They are psychological anchors. They help your brain switch from distraction to intention. Here's why:

1. Cognitive Anchoring - In psychology, anchoring is the process of linking meaning to a specific image, phrase, or sensation. A rune lets say, Algiz for protection becomes a trigger for a state of calm or clarity when practised regularly. It's similar to how a wedding ring symbolises commitment. Runes aren't just old symbols. They are anchoring tools that give your brain a shortcut to focus.

2. Pattern Recognition and Meaning-Making - The human brain is wired and loves to out seek patterns. When we assign meaning to a rune, we engage the default mode network. The part of the brain involved in memory, reflection, and self-understanding. Runes tap into this system, helping you link feelings, challenges, and intentions to visual representations and process them more effectively.

3. Neuroplasticity in Action - When you consistently use runes in meditation or reflection, you reinforce certain neural pathways. Especially those related to attention, calm, and self-awareness. This is called neuroplasticity: your brain's ability to change and adapt through repeated practice. Every time you trace a rune with intention, pair it with a breath, or reflect on its meaning. You are literally reshaping your mental habits.

Still Not Convinced? That's Okay. Mindfulness doesn't demand belief. It invites practice.

Your "Reset" in Practice

Encouragement to make mindfulness part of work life

Integrating mindfulness into the workplace is not about slowing down—it is about enhancing performance. When employees adopt mindful practices, they improve concentration, reduce stress, and make clearer, more strategic decisions. This leads directly to better productivity, stronger teamwork, and reduced burnout. Encouraging mindfulness at work positions businesses to thrive in fast-moving markets by building resilience and adaptability across their teams. Far from being a "soft skill," mindfulness is a competitive advantage that equips both individuals and organisations to perform at their best.

If this pocket guide has sparked something for you, know that it's just the beginning. Each rune carries layers of wisdom that can support not only your mindfulness but also your decision-making, resilience, and creativity. To explore further, I invite you to go deeper with the full book *Runes for Mindfulness*, join one of my workshops for practical guidance, or use the companion journal to make the practice your own. For those who prefer digital tools, the upcoming app offers daily rune draws and mindfulness prompts at your fingertips. Whichever path you choose, you'll find a way to weave these ancient symbols into modern life in a way that's meaningful and sustainable.

Visit https://celticstaggiftware.com/product-category/books/ to get your copy today.

Final Message

Mindfulness is not a destination, it is a daily practice. A way of living that allows you to step out of reaction and into presence. By incorporating even the smallest pause into your workday or personal life, you create space for better decisions, stronger resilience, and deeper clarity. My hope is that this guide has given you both the inspiration and the tools to begin. Or, to deepen your journey. Remember, you don't need to change everything at once. Start with one breath, one moment, one mindful step, and let the practice grow with you.

Further Reading/Other Resources

Runes for Mindfulness: A Simple Guide to Inner Peace
This book expands on the concepts in this pocket guide, taking you deeper into the history, symbolism, and practical use of Elder Futhark runes as tools for self-awareness, focus, and calm in a busy world.

Runes for Mindfulness Journal
A companion to *Runes for Mindfulness*, this journal provides guided prompts, rune reflections, and writing space to help you integrate mindfulness practices into daily life.

FURTHER READING/OTHER RESOURCES

Stop Defending: An Emotional Self-Defence Guide

A practical handbook for handling emotional bullying and unhealthy dynamics, this guide teaches you how to stop falling into defensiveness and instead respond with strength, clarity, and composure. It includes strategies, worksheets, and practical exercises for building emotional resilience.

How I Failed at Network Marketing to Succeed in Life

Part memoir, part life lesson, this book shares my journey through the ups and downs of network marketing. It's about finding success beyond failure—how embracing mistakes, learning from setbacks, and staying true to yourself can ultimately lead to a more authentic and fulfilling life.

www.ingramcontent.com/pod-product-compliance
Lightning Source LLC
Chambersburg PA
CBHW020547080526
44583CB00013B/1029